OKLAHOMA

OKLAHOMA

PHOTOGRAPHS BY DAVID FITZGERALD • TEXT BY BILL BURCHARDT

GRAPHIC ARTS CENTER PUBLISHING COMPANY
PORTLAND, OREGON

International Standard Book Number 0-912856-57-2
Library of Congress Catalog Number 79-92730
Copyright© 1979 by Graphic Arts Center Publishing Co.
P.O. Box 10306 • Portland, Oregon 97210 • 503/224-7777
Designer • Robert Reynolds
Printer • Graphic Arts Center
Typography • Paul O. Giesey/Adcrafters
Binding • Lincoln & Allen
Printed in the United States of America
Second Printing

1879-1935
To Oklahoma's beloved Native Son,
America's Ambassador to the World,
Will Rogers.

Page ii: Fallen leaves signal the arrival of fall as they
drift across isolated pond in southeastern area
of Delaware County.

Page 5: Windmill on horizon appears poised to
accept approaching rain shower north of
Black Mesa State Park.

The setting sun is partially obscured by evening haze west of Elk City. Left: Aerial view of plowed field reveals precision of tractor operator, northeast of Fairview. Pages 8 and 9 following: Setting sun bathes eastern shore of Lake Watonga during a thunderstorm in Roman Nose State Park. Park was named for last warrior chief of Cheyenne Indians, Henry Roman Nose.

Old farmhouse stands as a monument to role agriculture has played in the economic growth of this state. In 1975, it became for the first time, the number two industry in gross sales.

Late afternoon sunlight accentuates the rugged
surface and inside formation of Dakota
sandstone in Black Mesa area.

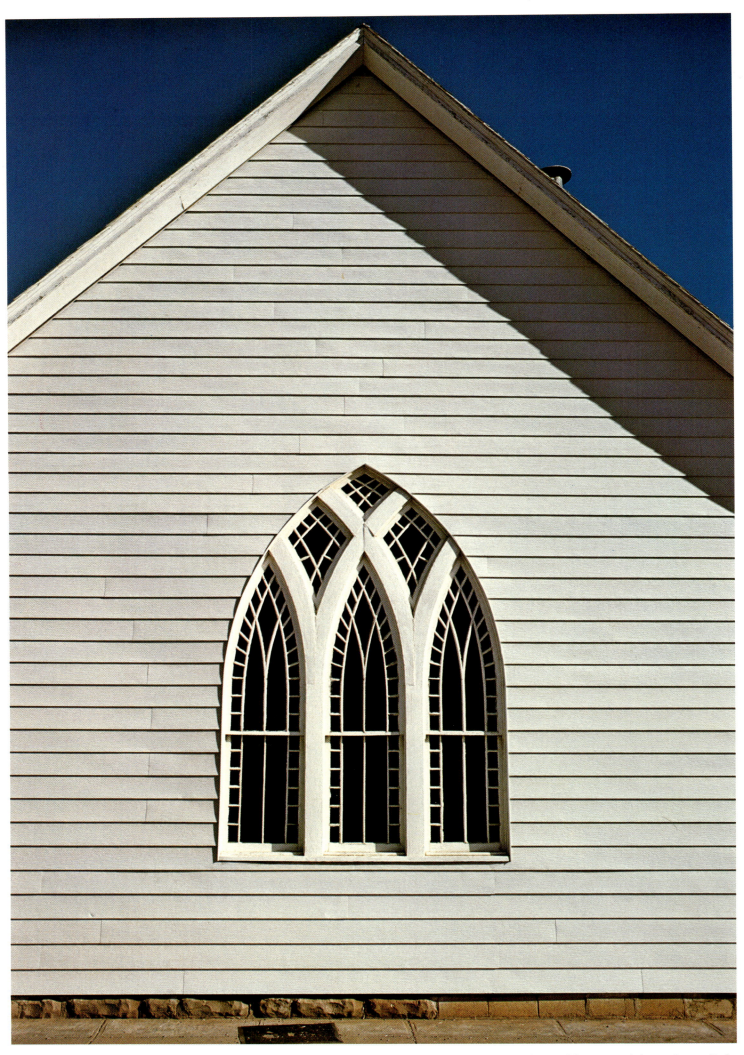

Gothic window adds a graceful touch to a little church in Dover. This small agricultural community was once known as Red Fork Station on the historic Chisholm Trail.

Tumbling water falls provide a change of pace,
in spring-fed canyon of Roman Nose State Park.

Reflections on Great Salt Plains Reservoir north of Jet. An 8,890 acre lake was created in 1941 with construction of 68 foot high dam across Salt Fork of the Arkansas River.

Ann Howard, No. 1 drilling rig, designed to
reach a depth exceeding 20,000 feet in
search of natural gas. It stands
slightly west of Elk City.

Swimmers enjoy the refreshing pool at base of
77 foot high Turner Falls in the Arbuckle
Mountains, largest water drop in state.

Swirling sunlit clouds aftermath of heavy
rainstorm, hover over Lake Carl Etling,
in Black Mesa State Park.

Sunrise is imminent along the horizon of western Arkansas. View looking east from Emerald Vista in the Ouachita National Forest. Right: Aerial of Great Salt Plains covering an area approximately seven miles long and three miles wide. Early Indian tribes gathered salt here and hunted, for the saline expanse drew an abundance of wildlife.

Elk enjoy the protective measures within
Wichita Mountains Wildlife Refuge. The Fish
and Wildlife Service which now administers
the park, is considering restricting some
recreational use now permitted. Left:
Looking south from the isolated Antelope
Hills northwest of Cheyenne. They were
a landmark for travelers on the California
Trail that crossed this region in the
mid-19th century.

Sika deer grazing on the lake-studded grounds surrounding the Woolaroc Museum. Located 14 miles southwest of Bartlesville, this 4,000 acre estate was once the country home of Frank Phillips, co-founder of Phillips Petroleum Company.

Conifers appear determined to survive on the
face of sheer sandstone wall near Wilburton.
Pages 24 and 25 following: Camera records
drift fence in far western Oklahoma,
near the Texas panhandle border.

Pioneer Woman, bronze statue on base of
native limestone, dedicated at Ponca City,
on April 22, 1930. Memorial to women who
created homes in virgin land on the frontier.

Cedar Canyon marks the entrance to Alabaster
Caverns State Park south of Freedom. This
ancient cavern is traversed by a 2300-foot long
trail through tunnels of white stone,
alabaster, and transparent crystals of selenite.

Brilliant spring blooming prickly pear cactus in Quartz Mountain State Park. Right: Lone maple tree emblazoned with autumn foliage along Elk Mountain trail in Wichita Mountains Wildlife Refuge.

Billy Creek projects a refreshing sensation as it
gently flows through isolated valley in
Ouachita National Forest. Left: Mammoth
cypress tree, approximately 2,000 years old,
a landmark on grounds of historic Gardner
Mansion east of Broken Bow, measures
14 feet in diameter at ground level.

Aerial exposes broad expanse of fertile farm land near Fairview. This flat plain attracted agriculturally inclined Mennonite farmers who now prosper in the area. Right: Placid flow of the Cimarron River highlighted by late evening sun in Black Mesa area.

Nature trail, meanders through an upland
hardwood weald, near Horse Thief Springs in
Ouachita National Forest. Left: Aesthetic
structure of black willow adds contrast to a
carpet of lush spring wheat erupting from
fertile soil near Cowlington.

Graceful limbs of pine tree near Emerald Vista in Ouachita National Forest. Right: Dakota sandstone mini-mesas known as The Three Sisters, are typical of the numerous rock formations in the Black Mesa area.

Single leaf appears firmly entrenched in dense
grass at edge of brook, in Roman Nose State
Park. Left: Gas flare and giant drilling rig
in position west of Elk City. This area is over
the Anadarko Basin, rich in oil and gas.
Pages 40 and 41 following: Maple foliage
maximizes the beauty of autumn in
Wichita Mountains Wildlife Refuge.

Aerial reveals sharply defined mesa, one of many that form the Glass Mountains. These mountains are part of the Blaine Escarpment, a major gypsum formation extending across much of western Oklahoma.

Polished granite boulders guard entrance to
canyon in Wichita Mountains Wildlife Refuge.
This game preserve is now protecting herds
of bison, elk, antelope and Texas longhorns.

Glass-like surface of small pond is perfect
setting for autumn reflections in
southeast area of Delaware County.

Acres of maturing sunflowers may escape the
approaching thunderstorm west of Boise City.

Combine has harvested an abundant yield for
rancher in undulating wheat field,
east of Mount Baldy.

Nature, the master craftsman, proven by
unusual rock formation in Quartz Mountain
State Park.

Restored and rebuilt home of Choctaw Chief
Thomas LeFlore, initially erected in 1837.
Located near Swink, it is considered to be the
oldest house still standing in the state.

Wildflowers render a change of pace in an arid
area near the New Mexico, Colorado border.

Flowering dogwood adds a graceful touch to pristine beauty of Dripping Springs Creek near Flint.

Ruins of barrack buildings at Fort Washita,
constructed in 1843. Founded by General
Zachary Taylor, this aged military post served
with distinction for nearly 20 years.

Butterfly at rest on large wildflower blossom
in field near Tishomingo.

Restored mansion of Jefferson Gardner, a
prominent Choctaw leader. It was erected
near the Arkansas border in 1881.

Ominous storm clouds dictate the arrival of a
severe thunderstorm in mid-afternoon
over Black Mesa area.

Tip of pine branch in Honor Heights Park,
Muskogee, recognized as one of top ten
municipal parks in the U.S.A. Pages 56 and 57
following: Perhaps the approaching storm is
ignoring the traffic sign over Black Mesa area.

Morning sunrise tends to reduce the winter
chill, northeast of Tahlequah.

Bitting Springs Mill covered with winter's mantle, near Stilwell. It is the state's last surviving water-powered grist mill established before the Civil War.

Redbud, the state tree, enhances this idyllic
setting near Sequoyah's home, northeast of
Sallisaw. Right: Unusual rock formation
in Robbers Cave State Park near Wilburton.
Reputed to have provided a camping place for
Belle Starr, the James brothers, and other outlaws.

Maple foliage reveals a seasonal change in
Red Rock Canyon near Hinton. Left: Early
morning view from Elk Mountain Trail
toward French Lake, in Wichita Mountains
Wildlife Refuge.

Looking east from Mt. Baldy, 6,260 acre
Altus Reservoir is partially visible. Nearby is
Quartz Mountain State Park.

Clear streams, numerous lakes, and granite
outcroppings are prominent land features of
the Wichita Mountains.

Barracks building at Fort Wichita is example of restoration by Oklahoma Historical Society. Left: Memorial to riders of the range, sculpted by Constance Warren. Standing near south entrance to capitol building, it was unveiled in 1930. Flags of Great Britain and Spain adjoining statue, are replicas of 14 different standards that have flown over the state in the years since 1541.

Snow and morning sun provide an aura of
brilliance on the Illinois River, in Cherokee
country. Right: Winter blankets even
the trees along the eastern shore of
Lake Hefner, northwest of Oklahoma City.

The bulb-shaped domes quickly identify
Russian Orthodox Church in Hartshorne. Left:
Field of brilliant yellow flowers in Beavers
Bend State Park, north of Broken Bow.
Pages 72 and 73 following: Towering
buildings mark the downtown skyline of
Oklahoma City, indicative of growth
prevailing in this capital city.

Aftermath of thunderstorm permits sunlight to bathe surface and shore of Lake Carl Etling in Black Mesa State Park. Right: April blooming hedgehog cactus in mountain area southwest of Quartz Mountain Lodge.

Last light of day renders a silhouette of downtown Tulsa, in heart of major oil producing region. It is America's westernmost inland port city on the Arkansas River navigation system. Left: Moisture-laden fog lies near the mirror-like surface of the **Mountain Fork River**, north of Broken Bow.

Unique rock formation discovered in Robbers
Cave State Park near Wilburton. Right: Frog
pondering his next leap along the Illinois River
near Chewey Bridge. This free flowing,
109 miles long stream, is fully protected
by action of the state legislature.

Full thrust of thunderstorm appears to be
approaching Castle Rock in Cimarron County.
It is only county in the United States that
borders on four states. Left: Gleaming grain
elevators soar skyward in fertile farming area
near Orienta. This tiny community lies on
the south bank of the Cimarron River.

Sunset casts an eerie glow over 46,500 acre Grand Lake of the Cherokees, seen below bridge north of Grove. Sprawling across three counties, this octopus-like lake backs up the waters of the Grand River. Right: Unusual beauty of entrance to Bizzell Memorial Library denotes symbol of academic excellence at the University of Oklahoma, Norman. It was established in 1892.

Canyon wall reflection on mirror-like surface
of small pond in Red Rock Canyon near Hinton.
Left: Firmly anchored limb, is ideal support
for coils and horizontal strands of barbed
wire on ranch near Reed.

Early risers on an excursion across Oologah Reservoir. This 5,850 acre lake was created in 1963, after completion of a 129 foot-high dam across the Verdigris River.

Setting sun fills the sky with color over Lake Murray. Pages 88 and 89 following: Delicate beauty of Price Falls offers a haven for relaxation in eastern area of Arbuckle Mountains.

Magnificent field of spring wheat,
blankets soil of Mound Valley southeast
of Weatherford in Caddo County.

Granite hills varying from 600 to 800 feet in
height dot the area in and around Quartz
Mountain State Park. Cedar, mesquite, and a
variety of oak cover the hillsides, providing
shelter for birds and small game.

Looking south from nearby Colorado border, the state's highest point, 4,973 foot, Black Mesa comes into view. In foreground, North Carrizo Creek destined to eventually join the Cimarron River.

Ribbon of pavement lies perfectly straight
across the treeless terrain east of Mooreland.
It is a segment of State Highway 15.

Splitlog church erected by Mathias Splitlog
nine miles northeast of Grove. A remarkable
Wyandotte Indian migrating here after his
birth in Canada, in 1812. This generous soul
underwrote all costs for its construction.

Indian Mounds near Spiro represent one of the
country's most significant archaeological
discoveries. Artifacts removed from these
mounds have become part of private
collections and museum displays in
Oklahoma and around the world.

Gnarled cypress tree, reeling from alternating weather cycles, appears determined to emulate survival on 2,175-foot King Mountain.

Blazing star, bud and blossom, dictate the arrival
of spring along nature trail in Robert S. Kerr
Arboretum, south of Poteau.

Reconstruction facsimile of o-si and
council house at historic Cherokee Village,
Tsa-La-Gi, near Tahlequah in Cherokee
County. Cherokee Indians have lived in
this county since their arrival in 1828.

Early evening sunlight casts an aura of brilliance over the Cimarron River near Black Mesa. Except for its beginnings in New Mexico and a brief foray into Kansas it is an Oklahoma River throughout its 395 mile length.

Setting for well preserved chapel and cemetery
expresses a feeling of peace and serenity
west of Watonga. Right: Ancient petroglyphs
on sheer rock formation in Black Mesa area
near isolated community of Kenton.

Cypress trees clearly visible above low-hanging
fog near surface of Mountain Fork River
in Beaver Bend State Park. Left: Farm structures
and windmill form a near-perfect silhouette
west of Slapout. Pages 104 and 105 following:
Mid-winter storm envelops flood plain of the
North Canadian River northwest of Jones.
Here in 1832 occurred the famed "Ringing the
Wild Horse" celebrated by Washington Irving
in his *Tour on the Prairies*.

Azaleas at the peak of their blooming cycle in Honor Heights Park. The staggering beauty of some 22,000 plants in park are recognized annually with a mid-April Festival. Right: Dominating entrance to the Will Rogers Memorial, stands the familiar Jo Davidson bronze of the slouched, hands-in-pockets humorist. Erected in Claremore, the memorial built and maintained by the state, contains the tombs of Will, his wife, and infant son.

Sea of wheat is result of the ideal growing
conditions that prevail in area west of Quartz
Mountain. Left: Awe-inspiring rotunda of
Capitol building embellished with four murals
by Charles Banks Wilson. They were dedicated
on Oklahoma Day, November 16, 1976.

The capitol building in Oklahoma City is a symbol of beauty, designed by English architect Wemyss Smith and S. A. Layton. The state was admitted to the Union in 1907 and building was completed in 1917. Right: Mid-afternoon sun highlights Indian paintbrush near sprawling Lake Texoma, one of the world's largest man-made lakes.

Blossom on prickly pear cactus reveals the
delicate beauty of this magnificent desert
flower. The root structure also aids in
stabilization of the soil that prevails north
of Black Mesa State Park. Left: Aerial captures
broad expanse of rugged terrain that shapes
the Glass Mountains. In the distance is
Lone Mountain, a landmark near Orienta.

Unique boulder formation discovered within
Wichita Mountains Wildlife Refuge. This 59,020
acre refuge was established by President
Theodore Roosevelt in 1905. Right: Fall foliage
drifting leisurely on surface of crystal clear
Dripping Springs, near Flint.

Aerial view reveals broad expanse of sand dunes several miles southeast of Little Sahara Recreation Area in Woods County. Nearly devoid of vegetation, they are constantly changing with the wind. Left: Honey Creek meanders down the face of Arbuckle Mountains to eventually join the Washita River. The formation of these mountains is an index to the geological makeup of the south-central area of the state.

The dinosaur, making its way through the giant-leafed tropical bush, paused in silent, reptilian vigilance. It swung its scaly armored head to survey downstream, then upstream, with the instinct of a hunter knowing that in an instant it can become the hunted.

A carnivorous allosaurus, it crossed the stream before it and continued on to disappear from sight in the steaming jungle on the far bank. The huge, clawed tracks it left in the viscous mud of the stream bed remained there, clearly visible. Pleistocene Oklahoma saw creatures that modern Oklahoma does not. These actual tracks of the allosaurus have, over the centuries, hardened into stone in the stream bed. They are still there today, visibly marking that dinosaur's passage across Carrizo Creek, near Kenton, in the Oklahoma panhandle.

During prehistoric ages panhandle Oklahoma was a tropical jungle, on the shores of a huge, inland sea. There lived the brontosaurus, pterodactyl, triceratops, the incredible creatures of cretaceous times. Their bones are still there. They have been found in dinosaur graveyards like the petrified forest on Robbers Roost Mountain, and unearthed from lone burials such as the one at our Dinosaur State Monument.

Tracks of prehistoric creatures abound among the rocks along the streams. Monster dinosaur eggs, now petrified, have been found. Petrified woods and tropical fruits are collected, cut and polished by hobbyist lapidaries, and decorate gem and mineral shows of Sooner rockhounds.

The prehistory of Oklahoma is a continuing source of new discoveries. Prehistoric carvings on canyon walls along the upper Cimarron, not far from the dinosaur tracks, have been identified and translated by Harvard professor emeritus Dr. Barry Fell. The carvings are in the ancient Iberian Punic language, Celtic Ogam, Phoenician, and Libyan. They represent the sun goddess Tanit of Carthage and Cádiz, reporting the arrival there of the "Bark of the Sun," from those venerable Mediterranean ports.

Another such discovery is a memorial carved to *Bhab*, son of *Mo*, member of a Celtic exploring expedition that had ascended the then navigable Cimarron to this point, millenia before the coming of Christ. *Meado Mahan* (Bear Hound), explorer from ancient Gaul, carved his name here. Carved boundary markers set out the land claimed by *Rata*, one of the Libyans.

There were many voyages to this continent in the centuries before Columbus set out to sea in 1492. Voyages by Mediterranean peoples, by Vikings from the Norselands, by the Chinese. Relics of many of these voyages have been found along the rivers, the waterways of ancient travel, in Oklahoma.

An aged-in-the-earth statue of the Ming dynasty Chinese god *Shu Shing Lao* has been excavated from the banks of the Deep Fork River, in central Oklahoma. In southeast Oklahoma, alongside the Poteau River, stands a giant stone on which Norse runes are carved. Viking carvers incised on it the date they erected it, November 11, 1012. Antiquities scholar Gloria Farley, of Heavener, has given a life of study to this runestone, carvings of ancient ships, and other petroglyphs found along our rivers.

The date, 1541, carved in an Oklahoma stone, marks the panhandle crossing of Spanish conquistador Francisco Vásquez de Coronado. Coronado's expedition camped at Castle Rock, alongside the Cimarron, on a trail much used from earliest Indian times. One of the two Italian members of the Coronado Expedition, either Bartolomé Napolitano or Francisco Roxoloro, carved his leader's name and the date, 1541, inside a small cave in the Castle Rock.

Historians are sure it was carved by one of the two Italians for he used the Italian spelling of the name, *Coronatto*. It is the earliest known European carving within the borders of the United States, and establishes European presence here almost a century before the Pilgrims landed at Plymouth Rock. Three centuries after Coronado passed by, the same route became the Cimarron cut-off of the Santa Fe Trail.

A most striking feature of Oklahoma's terrain is that it changes completely as it crosses the state. Cypress bayous, woodland pine forest, deciduous oak, gum, honey locust, sycamore, dogwood, redbud, sassafras, hickory, pecan, walnut, and other hard woods characterize our eastern border. The Kiamichi Mountains, the Winding Stairs, the Jackforks, the Cooksons and other mountains and hills range north through our Ozark Uplift, gradually giving way to the rolling hills of central Oklahoma.

These nurture the famed Crosstimbers, which run southwest from our northern border across the central part of the state. In places still impenetrable by man or horse, this forest of blackjack, post oak, and hickory is laced with wild vines, creepers, poison ivy and thorny greenbrier. Along the creek beds are canyons in which towering cedars, cottonwoods *(los álamos del río)*, and hardwoods grow, interspersed with groves of colorful sumac and tasty (after frost) persimmons.

Oklahoma's western border is semi-arid desert. The high plains prevail with all their variety of cactus, mesquite, sage, buffalo and curly grama grass. Salt cedar and willow mark the arroyos and water courses.

Sometimes changes of terrain occur sharply. Bromide Hill in the Chicksaw National Recreation Area has America's eastern woodlands on one side, and semi-arid southwestern desert on the other. In Red Rock Canyon in western Oklahoma, a sub-climate exists. The plateau which surrounds the canyon is arid; but the moist sub-climate along the floor of the 30 mile long canyon is reminiscent of New England, with tall maple trees in which orioles nest.

Oklahoma has been principally shaped by two factors: its variety of terrain, and the variety of the ethnic threads woven into our development. Early accounts written by European explorers and American pioneers list Kiowa, Comanche, Wichita, Lipan Apache, and Caddo among the indigenous people living here. Other Indian tribal groups came to Oklahoma during the 1800s, many of them purchasing land here from their own tribal funds. These were tribes moved here by "Indian Removals" that are a blot on our nation's past, but the glory of Oklahoma's history.

Death and intermarriage have eliminated some of the smaller remnant tribes—the Missouria, the Cayuga, for example—but 52 distinct tribal groups still reside in Oklahoma, each with a living language. More languages are spoken here than exist on the European continent.

Add then the immigrant groups who came to establish cattle ranches, to drill for oil, to mine the coal, or participate in the great Land Runs that opened this country to settlement; we have German, Czech, Mexican, Russian, Italian, African, Jewish, Greek; many of these national and ethnic groups hold festivals, so whatever your heritage, you are apt to find your language spoken and your customs and folkways celebrated somewhere in Oklahoma.

The changing patterns of human occupation in Oklahoma begin with pre-historic big game hunters who, with spear and atlatl, stalked the mammoth, mastodon, and other animals now extinct; several thousand years of this before the big game hunters, Clovis man and Folsom man, departed. Primitive agriculturists, at first only gatherers and storers of nature's bounty, learned at last to sow and cultivate their harvests. Traces of pre-historic irrigation ditches have been found in our panhandle, where they drew water from the Beaver River and the Cimarron.

Some of these ancient irrigation *acequias* were cleared and reopened by pioneer settlers. They are still in use today. For centuries prior to the coming of Europeans, the fertile, alluvial soil spread along our streams by primordial floods produced crops for ledge and cave dweller cultures. These primitive farmers stored their produce in intricately handmade baskets, bark containers, stone-lined caches, pouches of animal flesh and, eventually, pottery.

The finest of these cultures were the Mound Builders, who reached their zenith near Spiro. Much of the treasure trove of art objects they left to us was ruined by dynamiters and looters who avidly ripped the ancient mounds open. But many striking things remain, in museums and private collections; Spiro textiles woven of feathers, rabbit fur and buffalo hair, carved conch shell cups, sculptured animal and human figures, weaponry, copper adornments, all artistically equal to those found in Meso-America.

Dr. Joseph Mahan speculates that the Spiro builders and artists were Tula people, descended from the same Sumerian ancestors as the Toltec and Mayan cultures of Mexico. Winged and feathered serpents, Quetzalcoatl or Kukulkán, are frequent themes. The site and reconstruction of the Spiro mounds, adjacent to a most modern development—the Mayo lock and dam on the beautiful Arkansas River Waterway—make a remarkable combining of the ancient and the newest. As with the Maya cities, no one knows the cause of the collapse of the Spiro culture. Both declined, fading concurrently, just prior to the Spanish conquest of Mexico.

Vásquez de Coronado's passage through Oklahoma provided the curtain opening for our recorded history. He left behind Friar Juan de Padilla who, with lay brothers Sebastián and Lucas and the Portuguese soldier Andrés do Campo, hoped to Christianize the Wichita Indians. Enroute to visit the nearby Kaws, Friar Padilla was killed by Indians. The remaining three chose to return to New Spain. They were five years on the trail, wandering across central Oklahoma, finally reaching the Spanish colony near present Tampico.

An expedition led by Juan de Oñate entered western Oklahoma in 1601. Don Diego del Castillo came to the Wichita Mountains in 1650 to search for gold. Hernando de Soto approached Oklahoma, his expedition reaching Hot Springs, Arkansas, then turning south.

French competition for Oklahoma began in 1682, when Robert Cavalier, Sieur de la Salle, claimed it as a part of the Louisiana Territory. Bernard de la Harpe, with his aide, du Rivage, visited Indian towns along the Canadian River in eastern Oklahoma in 1719. Claude du Tisne traveled to the settlement called Ferdinandina in north central Oklahoma that same year. Pierre and Paul Mallet came through on the Arkansas River in 1740. Fabry de la Bruyere, in command of a group of French soldiers and traders, wintered on the Canadian River twenty-some miles southwest of present Eufaula, in 1741.

The French were winning, for in 1759 Diego Ortiz Par-rilla tried to sieze by armed force two villages, San Bernando and San Teodoro, on the Red River. The Wichita Indian occupants of the villages, flying the French flag, repulsed the Spanish assaults on their log palisade fort. Yet the entire Louisiana Territory was soon ceded to Spain in 1763 by the Treaty of Paris. In 1800, France regained title in the Treaty of San Ildefonso.

The Louisiana Purchase of 1803 terminated the Spanish-French competition, for it made all of Oklahoma except the panhandle the property of the U.S.A. Oklahoma became the far southwestern frontier of our nation, confronting the border of what was then New Spain.

To protect us from the "foreigners" on the other side of that border, and to try to resolve Indian conflicts on this side of the border, Forts Gibson, Towson, Coffee, Wayne, Arbuckle, and Washita were established. It was from Fort Gibson that *Legend of Sleepy Hollow—Rip Van Winkle* author Washington Irving made *A Tour on the Prairies* with his friends, English naturalist Charles Latrobe, and the Italian Count Albert de Portales.

As America's non-Indian population expanded, racial fighting increased. Indians had always fought other Indians, and hard pressed minority tribes were either wiped out or sought refuge farther from their enemies. The struggles increased as European settlers and Indians warred against each other. So, in 1804, the United States Congress created the "Indian Territory" and authorized President Andrew Jackson to remove Indians to it. Some 67 tribes were removed from their homelands and settled among the indigenous tribes already here. Thus Oklahoma came to include such vastly differing Indian cultures as the Osage, Comanche, Quapaw, Wichita, Apache, Catawba, Cayuga, Huron, Kickapoo, Miami, Missouria, Modoc, Mohawk, Nez Percé, Oneida, Onondaga, Oto, Ottawa, Pawnee, Peoria, Piankashaw, Ponca, Seneca, Tonkawa, Tuscarora, Wyandotte, Yuchi, and the Five Civilized Tribes. These tribes differ from each other as much as Europeans differ from Asians, or Africans.

Indian removal involves complicated forces and motives, beyond generalization. The subject merits thorough study, rather than summarization, but the dominant recurring theme is tragedy; Indian inhumanity to other Indians, within the broader context of man's inhumanity to man.

Responsibility for the Five Civilized Tribes' (Cherokee, Choctaw, Chickasaw, Creek and Seminole) *Trail of Tears* is rooted in human greed, supported by government. These Five Tribes Indians were literate owners of homes, farms, livestock; some were wealthy. They were better educated and more cultured than the vandals who dispossessed them. The states where they lived simply passed laws allowing white citizens to take their property.

The Indians appealed to the United States Supreme Court. It ruled that such treatment was unconstitutional. President Andrew Jackson refused to enforce the Supreme Court decision. In the thievery and brutality of removal the Five Tribes were driven west by the army and hired "contractors." Inadequately clothed, starving, in bitter winter, they died by thousands.

Historians Dr. Angie Debo, Dr. A. M. Gibson, and Grant Foreman are among those who have recorded the stark brutalities of removal in utter frankness. If permitted to live, these Indian people often saw their homes set afire and burned as they fled, but they were frequently murdered. Unsafe steamboats, overloaded like cattleboats with Indians being shipped west by the government, sank with great loss of life. The Seminoles, who resisted most bitterly, made their removal cost dearly. Dr. Gibson records that each Seminole removed to the Indian Territory cost the government $6,500, and the army paid with the life of one soldier for every two Seminoles removed.

The Plains Tribes already in the territory resented the arrival of the Five Civilized Tribes. War broke out between Osage and Cherokee. The Osage had come to Oklahoma early, under the aegis of the Chouteaus. In 1796 this French family began trading in the Three Forks country, where the Neosho, Verdigris, and Arkansas Rivers join. They founded a permanent trading post at La Saline, now Salina, in 1802. Here the Osages came to trap the plentiful mink, fox, wild cat, raccoon; a steamboat load of their furs shipped from Fort Gibson in 1824 included 300 female bear, 387 beaver, 670 otter, 770 cats and 3,000 deer skins. Comanches fought Choctaws and Chickasaws, causing the Red River Valley to be called "scalp alley." Troops from Fort Washita at last secured a precarious peace. Both cavalry and infantry occupied western Oklahoma, at Fort Sill, Fort Reno, Fort Supply, Camp Auger, and Camp Radziminski, in an effort to keep peace among the Indians, protect trails, waterways, and to facilitate further settlement.

The Five Civilized Tribes enjoyed a time of solid growth during the years just prior to the Civil War. Each tribe, an independent republic under its own constitution, established schools and maintained order with its own Indian police. The Cherokees, literate through the genius of Sequoyah, published their newspaper the *Cherokee Advocate*, books, and pamphlets, at Park Hill near Tahlequah.

Sequoyah is the only individual known in world history to have developed an alphabet or syllabary single-handed and working alone. His talent helped inspire not only his own people but the Creeks, Choctaws, Chickasaws, and Seminoles toward higher education, and the Five Civilized Tribes remained in the van of human progress.

The Civil War interrupted that progress. The War Between the States was fought in microcosm in Oklahoma, splitting the Five Tribes tragically in fratricidal fighting. Part of the Cherokees, Seminoles, and the Creeks remained loyal to the Union, others joined the Confederacy. Many of the Indians were themselves slave holders and plantation operators. But the real seed from which intra-tribal antagonism grew was not so much pro- or anti-slavery. Slaves among the Indians enjoyed great freedom, intermarried, and became equal participants in tribal affairs. It was antagonisms between the full-blood and mixed-blood factions that were at the root of every tribal cleavage. The full-bloods sought to cling to old ways; the mixed-bloods moved toward progress and change. Yet the leader of the Cherokee full-blood faction was John Ross, himself of mixed-blood. Patterns of factional loyalty often became blurred, but discord always remained strong.

The very last Civil War general to surrender was General Stand Watie, commander of the Cherokee Mounted Rifles. He surrendered at Doaksville, near Fort Towson on Red River, June 19, 1865, two months after General Robert E. Lee had surrendered at the Appomattox courthouse. Decisive battles were fought in Indian Territory. At the Battle of Honey Springs, near Muskogee, superior Union artillery and faulty Confederate gunpowder carried the victory for the Union. The Union steamboat J. R. Williams, loaded with provisions, uniforms, and medical supplies for Fort Gibson, was surprised and captured by General Watie's Confederate Indians in June, 1864. In September of that same year a rich supply train heavily guarded by Union troops was captured by General Watie's Cherokee Rifles on Cabin Creek. These rebellious activities of the Indians are difficult to understand, for in joining the Confederacy, they were fighting for the same southern states that had confiscated their lands and property only a few years before and driven them west over the deadly *Trail of Tears*. Further, their rebellion brought down upon them the wrath of the federal government, a wrath that made itself acutely felt in the Reconstruction following the war.

The victorious Union stated that, in seceding, the Five Civilized Tribes had violated their treaties. The United States called Indian leaders into conference at Fort Smith. Much negotiating eventually tempered and reduced Union demands, but the Indians who had joined the Confederacy provided leverage which permitted the federal government to abrogate all treaties. Reconstruction provided the excuse to take more Five Civilized Tribes lands on which to settle more Indian tribes, and further wedged open the way for colonization by white settlers.

The confusions of Reconstruction provided an opportunity for outlawry to get a strong foothold in the region. Frank and Jesse James, Cole Younger and his gang, Belle Starr, Cherokee Bill, Ned Christie, and the ruthless Buck gang took frequent refuge in the Indian nations and prospered. Upon his assignment as judge of the United States Court for the Western District of Arkansas, Isaac Parker then undertook to control this lawlessness. With the swearing in of competent and forceful deputies, like Bud Ledbetter and Heck Thomas, posses of marshals began to roam the Territory in caravans. Chaining their prisoners to the chuckwagon wheels at night, they brought in coveys of felons. At Fort Smith, malefactors found guilty of murder and rape were hanged. Parker acquired his nickname, "The Hanging Judge." His severity and the ruthlessness of the outlaws pursued provided the theme for much sensational fiction.

Reconstruction land taken from the Creeks and Seminoles was set aside as a reservation for the Cheyenne and Arapaho tribes. The Comanches, who had roamed here freely for centuries, were ordered by the Treaty of Medicine Lodge to confine themselves to terrain once the property of the Choctaws and Chickasaws. In similar actions the Wichitas, Caddos, Delawares, Keechis, Anadarkos, Ionies, Wacos, Kaws, Sac, Fox, Pottawatomies, and Iowas were assigned to other parcels of the former Five Tribes land.

Aggressive Kickapoo Indians had taken up residence in Coahuila, Mexico, and were raiding north into Texas. Colonel Ranald Mackenzie took his Fourth Cavalry into Mexico, captured as many as he could and brought them back to a reservation in the center of the Territory. The Osage people used their own tribal funds to purchase from the Cherokees what is now Osage County, the largest county in Oklahoma; beautiful rolling limestone hills rich with nutritious grasses. Successive generations of cattlemen leased Osage grass to fatten cattle for market. The Osage lands were later discovered to be rich in oil. During the early years of this century, until the oil reserves were depleted, the Osages were the most wealthy ethnic group in the world.

Final subjugation of the Kiowas provides a tale of mystery and bravery, that of Dó-ha-te the "Owl Prophet," Satank, and the feather that became a knife. In May 1871 a war party of Kiowa warriors rode south with Dò-ha-te.

Satank, a tired old man with a sparse mustache and one drooping eyelid, sought revenge for the death of his favorite son, killed on an earlier raid in Texas. The others, especially the young war chief Satanta, sought honor, booty, and coups. Dó-ha-te was a powerful medicine man. All were eager to harass white soldiers and settlers.

Their opportunity came when a party of soldiers passed the Kiowas while they lay in ambush. The "Owl Prophet" counseled patience. "Let them pass," Dó-ha-te's owl had cautioned. "Soon a wagon train of traders will come. Over them you will have great victory."

The party of soldiers included General Wm. Tecumseh Sherman, Commander-in-Chief of all U.S. armies. He was bound for Fort Richardson in Texas to investigate reports of Indian atrocities that had flooded his desk in Washington. The Kiowas took Dó-ha-te's advice. They let General Sherman and his small escort pass.

Hours later, the Kiowas were growing very impatient when the wagon train the owl had predicted at last appeared. It consisted of ten wagons, seven four-mule hitches and three pulled by six mules, freighting corn from Fort Richardson to Fort Griffin.

The Indians attacked. They killed seven of the freighters, counted many coups, took the possessions of their victims, and stole the mules. Five of the freighters escaped.

They fled to Fort Richardson, where General Sherman was present to hear the freighters' account of the destroyed wagon train. Sherman ordered pursuit. The trail led north, into the Indian Territory, to the Kiowa encampment at Fort Sill. There General Sherman went, to confront the Kiowa war chiefs. On the front porch of the commanding officer's quarters, they met in angry encounter. One of the war chiefs, Satanta, aggressively admitted his participation in the raid, bragging that he had led it. He named Satank and Big Tree, the war chiefs who were with him, but did not mention the medicine man Dó-ha-te.

The parade ground area around the porch was replete with Kiowa warriors and chiefs armed with bows and arrows, knives, carbines and rifles. Ranged facing them were the black buffalo soldiers of the Tenth Cavalry and Eleventh Infantry. Satanta met Sherman's charges with bitter countercharges regarding the slaughter of the buffalo, the Indians' commissary. The Kiowa said there was to be no more killing and jailing of Indians.

Bows were strung; rifles were pointed. Sherman demanded the return of the 41 mules stolen from the wagon train. A rattle of shots went off out-of-sight down the hill near the stone corral. One Kiowa and one soldier were killed there, nearly igniting the powder keg of confrontation on the commanding officer's front porch.

The Kiowas on the porch knew they were out-gunned and out-numbered. The army knew that should full violence erupt many would die, including their Commander-in-Chief, for many weapons were pointed at his heart. Word came that Kiowa women and children were taking flight, followed by a protecting rear guard of warriors.

Sherman ordered the arrest of Satanta, Satank, and young Big Tree. The three chiefs were marched off to confinement in a cellar guardhouse, and the impasse slowly broke up.

Satank was a member of the Ko-eet-senko, the Society of the Ten Bravest, accustomed to staking himself out in battle, to die where he had driven down his stake unless another member of the Ko-eet-senko came to release him. When the chiefs were securely loaded into sturdy wagons for transportation to Texas to be tried for murder, Satank staked himself out in the wagon that carried him.

He began to sing his death song and removed his handcuffs, scraping the skin from his hands in doing so. The Kiowas said he turned a feather into a knife, slashed at a soldier and took his rifle. Before he could use it effectively, bullets from many rifles cut him down.

Satank is buried where he fell, beneath a large elm tree, not far from Fort Sill's old parade ground. A native stone engraved to commemorate his courage marks his grave. Satanta and Big Tree were taken to Texas, tried, found guilty and imprisoned. Satanta committed suicide while in prison. Big Tree served until released from prison, then returned to his Kiowa people. He became a leader in trying to help them find and follow the white man's road. In his last years he served as teacher of a Bible class at Rainy Mountain Mission, and is buried in the cemetery there.

The inexorable forces of population growth and national expansion closed in on Indian people relentlessly. At the Battle of the Washita, General George Armstrong Custer fought the dress rehearsal for his death on the Little Big Horn. The Indians he attacked on the Washita were Black Kettle's Cheyennes.

Black Kettle's band had been overwhelmed by Colonel Chivington's militia at the Sand Creek massacre in Colorado. Black Kettle had brought the remaining few, in fear for their lives, to the Washita, seeking protection from Indian Agent W. B. Wyncoop at nearby Fort Cobb.

Custer hoped to win publicity as an "Indian Fighter," which would help him achieve his ambition to become President of the U. S. He led his Seventh Cavalry out of Fort Supply in the early winter of 1868. A forced march through a blizzard brought them to the Washita. Here they waited overnight in bitter cold and snow, stamping to keep their feet from freezing and holding fingers in their horse's mouths to keep them from whinnying. They attacked at dawn on November 27.

The Cheyennes were sleeping in their tepees. Custer attacked to the sprightly music of his regimental band, playing the Gary Owen. He split his troops just as he would later split his force in the attack at Little Big Horn. On the Washita, Major Elliot's troop was surrounded and killed to the last man. Custer escaped. On the Little Big Horn, Reno's split off troop escaped. Custer himself was surrounded and his command killed to the last man.

On the Washita, 102 of Black Kettle's warriors, women, and children were killed. Black Kettle and his wife were shot in the back as they tried to flee across the ice-choked stream. Custer ordered the Indians' horses slaughtered. More than 800 ponies were killed while Custer shot dogs for target practice. The camp's tepees, buffalo robes and winter food supplies were burned. Appropriating the finest robes for himself, the general then ordered the 57 women and children prisoners rounded up and the column set out for Fort Supply.

During the trip Custer took Monaseetah, daughter of Little Raven, to serve as his "interpreter." She spoke no English, only Cheyenne. Nine months after reaching Fort Supply, Monaseetah gave birth to a beautiful baby. She called the child Yellow Swallow. She had known Custer as Yellow Hair.

Among the last struggles of the Indian wars, Quanah Parker, Comanche son of Peta Nocona and his captured bride Cynthia Ann Parker, led a war party in attacking buffalo hunters at Adobe Walls in a futile effort to stop the killing of the buffalo. In 1874, raiding Indians overtook Pat Hennessey's wagon train near present Hennessey, Oklahoma. Four teamsters were killed and the wagon train sacked and burned. Pat, tied to a wagon wheel, burned to death.

The Indian Wars were over. The buffalo had been destroyed. The last recalcitrant warrior bands were captured and brought into the reservations. The chiefs were imprisoned at Fort Marion, Florida. Education at the Carlisle Indian School was undertaken for those who seemed tractable. Returning to Oklahoma they practiced the trades and skills they had learned. Among the Indian survivors, those of Geronimo's band were assigned land near Fort Sill. The town that grew up there is named Apache, known today for the fine Apache artists, artisans, farmers, and cattle ranchers who call it home.

The saga of steamboating merits surprising interest here for the state has always provided some of America's most fascinating watertrails west. A famed early traveler on the Arkansas River was the pirate Jean Lafitte. Disguised as "Captain Hillare" he brought the French cartographer Arsène Latour upriver in 1816 to map the frontier stream. Both were paid by the French, who used the maps Latour made to plan the defense of the river from the aggressive colonies of New Spain.

Early Indian traders who came up the river in pirogues were followed by flatboaters. These hardy voyagers constructed huge flatboats capable of carrying 300 or more tons. Loaded with furs, they floated down river to New Orleans to sell both furs and flatboat. If the lumber of which the flatboat was made was not likely to bring a sufficiently high price, they could load up with trade goods and head back upriver, poling, rowing, rigging a square sail, or cordelling it to Fort Gibson on the Arkansas River or Fort Towson on the Red River.

Travel by steamboat boomed after the Civil War, though it was always dangerous. Torrential spring and autumn rains tore great trees out of the river banks. Some of these were sure to lodge on the bottom with their jagged trunks pointed upstream, ready to rip the bottom out of the first passing steamboat.

Even worse than the snag was the "sawyer." A giant of the woodlands would hinge itself in the bottom sand and bow and scrape in the current. Out of sight beneath the surface, now lifting itself high out of the water, it was a monster capable of swamping the unwary, who often had no knowledge of its existence until too late.

Worst of all was the "raft." One log snagged on a sandbar piled up others behind it until a mass of them blocked the stream. Such a "raft" extended downstream on the Red River for 70 miles below Fort Towson. Captain Henry Shreve, for whom Shreveport is named, developed the ingenious snagboat that unsnarled this peril to navigation. Lifting out one entangled, gnarled rooted tree at a time, in five years of work he cleared away the great Red River Raft. Sternwheelers could ascend regularly to Fort Towson, and occasionally to Fort Washita, carrying passengers, mail, hardware, candles, rope, manufactured goods upriver, and bringing produce and raw materials down.

In the remote upper reaches of the Red River lived Zeb Marston. Zeb insisted that the captain of the mail steamer *Emperor* leave a barrel of whiskey at his cabin each and every week. It was troublesome to navigate the shallows up to Zeb's cabin. The captain of the mail steamer protested, asking why Zeb needed all that whiskey. Zeb

told him, rather hotly, "Way out here where I am the drinking water is bad, and I've got a sick wife, and *no cow.*"

Sam Houston, destined for fame in Texas, came up the Arkansas on the sternwheeler Facility, Captain Phillip Pennywitt, master, in 1829. Houston, fleeing the scandal of his recent marriage and immediate divorce in Tennessee, had come to spend a season with his close friend Chief Oo-loo-te-ka of the Cherokees. While living in Oklahoma, Sam Houston built Wigwam Neosho near Fort Gibson, and took as his consort the beautiful Cherokee Talihina Rogers. When he departed for Texas a few years later he tried to persuade her to go along, but she preferred her home on the Neosho.

Captain Pennywitt was *the* legendary steamboat master on the upper Arkansas. Port logs and chronicles of the times are full of his comings and goings; transporting cargo, towing keelboats loaded with Five Civilized Tribes people being removed to the Indian Territory. In contrast to the incompetent captains and the battered, decrepit steamboats whose sinkings cost the lives of so many during those tragic Trail of Tears days, Captain Pennywitt never lost a ship nor a passenger.

Capt. "Rich Joe" Vann, who ran a cotton plantation at Webbers Falls in the Indian Territory was ripe for such a disaster. He named both his gorgeous sidewheeler steamboat and his racing mare *Lucy Walker,* then indulged his passion by racing every horse or steamboat he encountered. He would order the Negro slaves on his steamboat to feed the boilers sides of bacon to heat the chimneys red hot. On one trip he took the *Lucy Walker* in to the bank to load passengers. As she moved back out into the stream, overloaded, her boilers blew up in terrible explosion. Captain Vann was killed. All the crew and passengers were killed or frightfully wounded. Investigating the tragedy, Lloyds of London determined that "Rich Joe" had stopped the *Lucy Walker's* engines to correct some minor malfunction and she had exhausted the water in her boilers.

Another steamboat explosion involved the superintendent for the Western Indians, a Captain Armstrong. Captain Armstrong had traveled to New Orleans to receive $150,000 in payments due the Cherokees. The steamboat returning him to Fort Gibson exploded. The paper money "in sturdy kegs bound by substantial hoops" floated off down the river. A box of gold coins he carried blew apart and the coins were scattered about the shore. A "box of dimes and half-dimes" flew into the air, then, rent asunder, fell on the steamboat's bow. By superhuman effort, Captain Armstrong recovered all but $61 of the paper money, and all but $90 of the gold coins, dimes, and half-dimes. A truly dedicated public employee, he guarded the money day and night until another steamboat came to take him on to Fort Gibson.

The romance and dangers of steamboating hold a high place in historic literature, as do the western cattle trails, the only method of delivering beef to a hungry market in the years immediately following the Civil War. The Chisholm Trail crossed Oklahoma from border to border enroute to the railhead at Abilene, Kansas. Texas cattlemen, often pooling several herds and all the mavericks they could brand, contracted a drover. Then with chuckwagon and cook, nighthawk, point, swing, and drag riders, the long drive was made across the Indian Nations.

Fierce Comanche, Kiowa, or Cheyenne tribesmen along the way were likely to demand a "wohaw" or two as crossing toll. The Indians had heard drovers shout the terms "whoa" and "haw" at the cattle, and thought this must be the name of the beasts being driven. Trail bosses were entranced with the lush grasses of this Oklahoma country. In the flood plains of the rivers, the Red, Washita, Great Canadian and the North Canadian, Blackbear, Kaskaskia, the salty Cimarron, and the Beaver, grass was so high they could tie it in knots over the withers of their cow ponies. So the cattlemen returned to Texas, gathered more cattle, and returned to establish ranches in our Cherokee Strip, in the Unassigned Lands, in the Big Pasture, and around the Quartz, Wichita, and Arbuckle Mountains.

Before the Chisholm Trail, the Shawnee Trail crossed eastern Oklahoma. It was shut down by Kansas farmers, because Texas cattle brought Texas fever. As the Kansas railhead moved west from Wichita to Dodge City the cattle trails moved west. After the Chisholm Trail came the Great Western Trail, through Woodward and Fort Supply; then the Jones and Plummer Trail, which passed directly through Beaver City's main street, then on to cross the Beaver River.

The era of the cattle trails spawned great turbulence. The railroads were eager to build south across the Indian Territory and Indian people knew railroads would bring droves of white settlers. Clashes followed; but the building of the Missouri-Kansas-Texas, the Santa Fe, the Rock Island, the Fort Smith and Western was inevitable. The coming of the railroads closed the cattle trails, made the steamboat obsolete, and signaled the end for the Indian reservations. The unique Oklahoma Land Runs resulted from railroad instituted pressures with, as a side effect, the escalation of outlawry.

The Doolin Gang, Bob, Grat, Bill and Emmett Dalton, Bittercreek Newcomb, Red Buck Weightman, Little Dick West, Black Face Charlie Bryant, Tulsa Jack, Dynamite Dick, Zip Wyatt, were men with colorful names and lurid reputations. Not infrequently they robbed, then, through adversity, lost their loot, which has made Oklahoma a state favored by hunters of buried treasure.

My interest in that subject fetched me a telephone call late one afternoon from an old gentleman who said, "I hear you're interested in buried treasure." He invited me to call on him. I found him in a room in one of Oklahoma City's skid row hotels. He was 84 years old. His false teeth were loose and clacked so badly it was difficult to comprehend his words, and he was secretive.

"I know where eighty thousand dollars is buried," he claimed.

"Where?" I asked.

"I don't dare tell you. They'd kill me."

"Why don't you go dig it up?"

"It's too hot," he insisted.

This kind of dialogue went on for sometime. He told me his name was Bus Hodge, that he had been a deputy marshal, a bodyguard for Maud Lee Mud at the time she was the world's richest Indian lady from her wells in the rich Maud oilfield. Hodge hinted that he was on intimate terms with several notorious riders of the owlhoot trail. As lawman and outlaw he had plainly worked both sides of the street, but the details he was willing to divulge were sparse and fragmentary.

He said the $80 thousand dollars had been buried in southeastern Oklahoma since 1926. The money was all in five dollar bills—not the small five dollar bills of today, but the big old greenbacks that were the currency of the 1920s. One of the outlaws who had stolen them was an

"Oklahoma boy." He wanted me to hire a few competent gunmen he knew who would help us and we would go and dig up the money.

All this seemed pretty fanciful, and I finally told him I was more interested in writing about buried treasure than in digging for it, and went on my way. A few weeks later, while doing research on another subject, I came upon an account of the robbery of the Denver mint—in the year year 1926. The sum of $160 thousand dollars was stolen in that robbery, all in five dollar bills, the big old greenbacks of the 1920s. Half the money was later recovered, but $80 thousand dollars of the loot was never found. One of the outlaws who had participated in the robbery was Harvey Bailey, a southeastern "Oklahoma boy" who had later taken part in the notorious Urshel kidnapping.

I hurried to the telephone and called the skid row hotel where Bus Hodge had been staying. He had checked out and departed, leaving no forwarding address. We hear much about buried treasure, but little about found treasure—for two reasons; found treasure is usually discovered on someone else's property, and the landowner invariably wants a healthy share of the treasure found; second, a heavy income tax has to be paid on found treasure.

When the Five Civilized Tribes came to Oklahoma many of their members were well-to-do, owners of slaves, livestock, and cash money. There were no banks here then. Surplus money was kept hidden. It was not uncommon for some old grandfather to die suddenly without revealing where his money was buried. One George Hardsook found $37 thousand dollars in gold coins some years ago while digging a gas pipeline ditch near Oglesby in Nowata County. He took the money into Rodecker's store to count it. The excited storekeeper went to get S. A. Utterstein, owner of the land on which the pipline ditch was being dug. When Rodecker and Utterstein returned to the store, Hardsook was gone and has never been heard from since.

To avoid sharing the money with landowners and the Bureau of Internal Revenue, finders of lost loot keep very quiet about their discoveries. There is hardly a town in Oklahoma where you cannot arrive, check in at a local motel, and in minutes ferret out a story of outlaw gold or buried treasure within an hour's drive of that town.

The passing of the cattle trails and the coming of the railroads were accompanied by the closing of the open range, settlers clamoring for the allotment of the Indian reservations, then the Land Runs. Reservation lands were held in common by the whole tribe. By forcing each Indian to accept an individual allotment of land, many millions of acres were left to be distributed by lottery, auction, and run to homesteaders.

First came the Run of '89. Land hungry settlers lined up around the boundaries of the unassigned lands in central Oklahoma. At noon on April 22, 1889, the starting guns of the soldier guards sounded, and everybody ran to seize a claim. Boomers made the run on horseback, in buggies, surries, farm wagons carrying their belongings and sometimes their families, or even on foot. An imaginative painting of the Cherokee strip Run has a Boomer riding a bicycle, but no authentic account of a bicycle rider racing to stake a claim has ever been verified.

Many a Boomer was disappointed to find a Sooner already roosting on the land he chose. These Sooners had slipped across the line in the dark of night. They hid in the canyons and draws until the noon signal for legal entry. Others, legally in the territory as railroad agents and such, staked claims to town lots or homesteads and simply took possession of them before anyone racing from the border could get there. Contests for "Soonered" claims were often settled in the courts.

Some Sooners already had a garden planted and growing. They aimed to stay, and frequently did, legally or illegally. Others only wanted a little easy money and were willing to "relinquish" their claims for a few dollars, or whatever they could get. At least one rancher had his cowboys stake claims, which he promptly bought. Each outlaw then riding with Bill Doolin "Soonered" a claim in the big bend of the Cimarron known as Cowboy Flat. Most of them had been cowhands for ranchers Harry and Oscar Halsell, and knew the country thoroughly.

The outlaws sold their relinquishments to the highest bidders. Dick Broadwell sold his, then hied himself off to Dallas with a pretty widow lady who had also sold her relinquishment. Dick kept enough money to buy himself a new suit, gave the rest to the pretty widow and sent her off to buy their marriage license and open a joint bank account for them. He never saw her again.

Though guns were often drawn in threatening gesture, no settler is known to have been killed in a claim dispute. In the Cherokee Strip Run of 1893, my grandfather bought a neighboring claim and gave it to the Sooner who came up out of hiding in a creek canyon. "Soonering" was considered contemptible by honest settlers. It merited the death penalty if the Sooner could be charged and convicted, but witnesses were scarce. It was simpler to settle the matter on the site. Settling a claim fight in court often took years, and a homesteader who killed a "Sooner" could be charged with murder.

Unallotted Cheyenne-Arapaho lands were opened by run, as were those of the Kickapoo. The Kiowa, Comanche, and other "surplus" lands, were opened by lottery. Hopeful settlers registered at Fort Reno, Fort Sill, etc., and a drawing was held. Registrants whose names were drawn were the lucky winners. The Big Pasture was opened by auction. One claim per bidder went under the hammer for an average of ten dollars per acre.

With the land openings, the Twin Territories, Indian Territory and Oklahoma Territory, were united. A symbolic wedding was held on the steps of the new Carnegie Library in the territorial capital at Guthrie. The Organic Act of 1890 gave Oklahoma her panhandle. This "No Man's Land" had been overlooked by Congress in the formation of all the states around it, to become known as the neutral strip, where no officer of law had any authority.

Sparsely settled ranchers in the neutral strip and townsmen, especially those of Beaver City, made an effort to organize the neutral strip into Cimarron Territory, with an aim toward separate statehood. But Congress would not agree, even though the State of Cimarron would have been larger than either of two already existent states, Delaware and Rhode Island.

Oklahoma's size is deceptive. The state is larger than Maine, New Hampshire, Vermont, Massachusetts, Connecticut, Delaware, and Rhode Island combined. Policing such an area in pioneer times was problematical. A few United States marshals, headquartered at Guthrie, undertook this chore. Led by intrepid men, such as the Three Guardsmen, Heck Thomas, Chris Madsen, and Bill Tilghman, a small posse would ride out to take on an organized gang, or follow the trail of a renegade loner.

Early day law enforcement was complicated by the fact that the boomtowns of the oil rush extended the Wild West over into the twentieth century for Oklahoma. Lewis Ross, brother of Cherokee Chief John Ross, brought in the first commercial oil well in the Indian Territory in July, 1859, more than a month before Colonel Edwin C. Drake brought in the "first commercial oil well" of record, near Titusville, Pennsylvania.

The Indian Territory Illuminating Oil Company was producing petroleum in the Osage country in the 1800s. Demands for oil soared after Henry Ford began making the Model T. Oil discoveries in Oklahoma then exploded in the media with the Golconda impact of the Klondike gold rush and Virginia City's Comstock Lode. Glenpool, the Osage oil rush, Drumright, Seminole, each new field meant the rapid booming of wild and wooly oil rush towns.

Those shallow, early oil fields permitted a man with little or no money to put together a stock company and drill for the big prize. Unpaved dirt roads of those times meant that workers must live where the drilling was going on. To each new discovery swarmed a horde of oil speculators, lease men, company executives and employees, drillers, tool dressers, and roughnecks, along with card sharks, bootleggers, prostitutes, the birds of prey who came to offer entertainment.

Towns like Kiefer, Whizbang, Ragtown, Bowlegs, Red Fork, Drumright, Damright, Dropright, Downright, Alright, and Justright sprang from zero to thousands in population over night. They ran wide open and full blast. The men came alone, to live in tents or jerry-built boarding houses, for the oil rush boomtown was no place for a family—no churches, no schools, and only gambling joints, saloons, and brothels for entertainment. Law enforcement was at first unwanted, but finally essential.

Bill Tilghman, buffalo hunter, and former marshal of cowtown Dodge City, was killed in 1924 at age 72, in the Oklahoma oil rush boomtown Cromwell, while he was arresting a United States prohibition officer charged with creating a drunken disturbance. Buck Garrett, who had been one of the "enforcers" hired by the cattlemen in Wyoming's Johnson County War, was the law in Carter County. These and other men in the same tradition, like Logan County's Indian Sheriff Milo Beck, fought the battles against lawless men as they had been fought in frontier towns throughout the earlier west of the prior century.

Seminole's Jake Sims never carried a gun, but he was shrewd and clever, had an amazing memory, and a near genius for crime prevention and sudden solutions. For example, a Seminole druggist hired a young pharmacist. The young man opened the drugstore one morning, removed the tray of narcotics from the safe and left it for a moment on top of the safe, while he walked to the front of the store to wait on a customer.

As the young pharmacist asked the customer, "May I help you?" Jake Sims walked in the front door and handed the pharmacist his tray of narcotics. An addict had slipped in the back door and stolen the narcotics while the pharmacist was walking to the front of the store. Jake Sims had been watching the addict from across the street, and relieved him of his booty as he exited the drugstore.

A Seminole jeweler, robbed one night, called Jake on the telephone to report the robbery as soon as he recovered his composure after the hold-up man had run out the front door.

"I was just about to call you," Jake told the jeweler. "That fellow who held you up will be getting off the bus in Henryetta in about 30 minutes. I've already called the Henryetta chief-of-police. He'll meet the bus, and if you'll drive on over there you can pick up your stolen property."

Any single one of Oklahoma's oil rushes produced more wealth than all the gold rushes in the American West combined. One 160 acre lease in the Three Sands field produced more than the entire cost of the Louisiana Purchase. In 1959 some 80,000 wells were producing oil and/or gas from 1,700 oilfields in 70 of Oklahoma's 77 counties. More than half of the state's total acreage was then under lease for future exploration, and nearly 100,000 Oklahomans were engaged in some branch of the oil industry. Now deep drilling in the Anadarko Basin and wildcat locations, predominantly in western Oklahoma, hopes to find oil and gas at much greater depths than the flush production fields now depleted.

But the stark fact is that we must mine our coal fields, pursue solar, wind, and nuclear energy, develop the laser for energy transmission from outer space, and all at optimum speed. America is running out of oil so rapidly that a few dire crisis confronts us unless there are quick and remarkable breakthroughs in other areas of energy production.

This is sharply evident to anyone who has grown up in Oklahoma. Throughout my youth and college years you could not drive in any direction without encountering a forest of derricks, at Three Sands, Roxana, Oklahoma City, Earlsboro, Cushing—young oilfields were everywhere. Now the forests of derricks are gone. These old oilfields are now pumped, or producing through methods of secondary and tertiary production. Water flooding forces water down into the rock formations to force out the last remaining oil from limestone and shales once so charged with gas pressure that the oil literally exploded from the earth. Then gushers and wild wells were commonplace.

Pumpjacks, called grasshoppers because they look like a grasshopper, and gun-barrels, a group of small tanks and a separator, dot the Oklahoma countryside. But the endless ranks of derricks that once dominated our skylines are gone. Occasionally one sees a distant wildcat, the towering derrick of an exploratory well. But the army of drilling rigs that marched across this land has passed on.

When the derricks disappeared, they left black earth as far as the eye could see. A scene more desolate can hardly be imagined. Thousands of acres of oil-soaked earth dotted with sparse black skeletons of defoliated blackjack trees, and creeks sluggish with waste oil and salt water. I recall looking at those wastelands and thinking *no blade of grass will ever grow here again.* But I was wrong. The earth has incredible regenerative powers. Now, where steam powered drilling rigs once barked like cannon fire, sometimes to strike black gold, always spreading black waste out from their slush pits, their gas waste flares lighting the countryside by night, there remains no sign that they were ever there.

The oil blackened earth has again become lush green pasture where cattle graze. The creeks flow transparently, their sandy beds clearly seen. Oak groves stand green in spring. Birds have sowed hillside cedars. The passing of 30 years has remade nature's prairie beauty. But it takes well over a million years for nature to make a new oilfield, necessitating an urgent program to find substitutes for the oilfields we have used up.

Cattle are important in Oklahoma. Agriculture is our number two industry, after oil and gas. Food and fiber production, cattle, sheep, hogs, milk, eggs, chickens, turkeys, wheat, cotton, peanuts, broom corn, oats, barley, rye, corn, cow peas, popcorn, mung beans, guar, spinach, green beans, milo and combine maize, cantaloupes, watermelons, alfalfa, vetch, sorghum . . .

An epic Soonerland agricultural enterprise was the Miller Brothers 101 Ranch near Ponca City. 101,000 acres, in large part leased from the Ponca Indian tribe, grazed 25,000 head of cattle. The ranch raised many of the crops just listed, had its own electric power plant, canning factory, cotton gin, tannery, cider mill, alfalfa mill, dairy, hogs, poultry, meat packing plant, community store, restaurant, and oil refinery. More, its 101 Ranch Wild West Show traveled the nation in 150 railroad cars carrying 126 cowboys, Indians, wild steers, horses, tents, parade wagons, calliope, banners and show equipment.

The 101 Ranch show launched Tom Mix, Buck Jones, Hoot Gibson, and William Desmond on movie careers. It encountered trouble while showing abroad in 1914. England entered World War I and took the show's livestock for the British army. Returning home with only a few of their valuable trained horses, the Miller family quit show business for a time, devoting full energy to their agricultural enterprises. In the 1920s, yielding once more to the lure of the sawdust ring, they purchased the Walter L. Main Circus, using its animals and properties to expand their new show, the 101 Ranch Real Wild West and Great Far East. Cowboys and Indians, now 1,400 of them, loaded the railroad cars again. The deaths of Joe and George Miller left brother Zack all alone, then came the depression of 1929. Now little remains of the 101 but memories.

Oklahomans have a host of great memories. Of Will Rogers to whom this book is dedicated. We celebrated the Centennial of Will Rogers' birth on November 4, 1979. In the 1920s and 30s he was the best known American in the world and the most beloved citizen of the United States. He made more than 70 movies and was the top box office star during his last full year in Hollywood. His columns were carried by 350 newspapers. A Ziegfeld Follies celebrity, he was paid $500 a minute for his radio speeches. Killed in Alaska in a plane crash with Oklahoma aviation pioneer Wiley Post in 1935, more than half-a-million visitors stop each year at the Will Rogers Memorial in Claremore to pay tribute to this humble Indian cowboy who lassoed our hearts.

Wiley Post discovered, developed, or tested and proved the effectiveness of the tools of modern aviation, the *automatic pilot,* the *radio direction finder,* the *variable pitch propeller.* His studies proved that man's limitations in air and space are not technological, but biological, that only the human *biological clock* limits what we can do in the wild blue yonder. Wiley discovered the *jet stream* and made the first use of it for fast, long distance flights. He made the first pressurized space suit, using it for *stratospheric flight.* Today's space suits are made using Wiley Post's patents. He was the predecessor of our astronauts, of whom Oklahoma has produced more than any other state; Gordon Cooper (Gemini 5), Thomas Stafford (Gemini 6-7, Apollo, Saturn 10), Stuart Roosa (Apollo 14), Owen Garriot (Skylab 3), William Pogue (Skylab 4), and Dr. Shannon Wells Lucid, our first woman astronaut.

We remember Indian athlete Jim Thorpe, Sac and Fox, who won both the pentathlon and decathlon in the 1912 Olympic Games. The King of Sweden gave him his medals with the comment, "Sir, you are the greatest athlete in the world." Which sports writers confirmed more recently when they named Thorpe the "athlete of the half century." World attention also focuses on our great Indian ballerinas. Osage Maria Tallchief of the American Ballet Theatre; her sister Marjorie Tallchief, long prima ballerina of the Paris Ballet; Rosella Hightower, Cherokee, prima of the Marquis de Cuevas Ballet; Yvonne Chouteau, Cherokee, Ballet Russe de Monte Carlo; Moscelyne Larkin, Shawnee-Peoria, also of the Russian Ballet. Yvonne and her *premier danseur* husband, Miguel Terekhov, now head the ballet school at Oklahoma University. Moscelyne and her *premier danseur* husband, Roman Jasinski, now direct Tulsa's Civic Ballet.

Kiowa Indian author Scott Momaday won the Pulitzer Prize for his novel *House Made of Dawn.* Cherokee Admiral Jocko Clark led us to naval victories in World War II, as did non-Indian Oklahoman Admiral Marc A. Mitscher. Osage General Clarence L. Tinker died in the Pacific, but his name lives on at huge Tinker Airforce Base, Midwest City, our nation's major air materiel center.

In the sports world there was Pepper Martin, who won the 1931 World Series almost single handed for the St. Louis Cardinals' Gashouse Gang. Johnny Martin won the sobriquet *Wild Horse of the Osage* for the reckless abandon with which he played football for the Hominy Indians, an all-Indian pro team from the small Oklahoma town of Hominy that beat the New York Giants, then champions of the National Football League (1927). When Johnny played baseball for the Cardinals he would put on his uniform, shoes, and cap—no sox, no underwear, no athletic supporter, no pads, no protective equipment of any kind, then take the field and play with the same wild abandon he had played football.

Sooner baseball greats include Paul and Lloyd Waner (Big Poison and Little Poison), Allie Reynolds, Warren Spahn, Dale Mitchell, Paul and Dizzy Dean (who were born in Texas, Louisiana, or Oklahoma, depending on which newspaper reporter they were talking to), Carl Hubbell, Mickey Mantle, Alvin Dark, Johnny Bench and others . . . some of them Indian and some not, for Oklahoma palefaces make the bigtime, too.

We're thinking of actors Van Heflin, Jennifer Jones, Buck Jones (a celluloid cowboy who was a real hero—he gave his life saving others in the Boston Cocoanut Grove fire of 1942). The greatest of all jazz trombonists, Jack Teagarden, grew up in Oklahoma City with his piano playing genius sister, Helen, and his trumpeter brother Charley. Charley and Jack achieved fame playing with Paul Whiteman. Jack, deceased, is buried in the jazz capital, New Orleans. Charley, the last we heard, was still leading the band at the Silver Slipper in Las Vegas.

Count Basie was just plain Bill Basie when he played piano with Oklahoma City's Blue Devils. He took the Blue Devils to Kansas City and, when Bennie Moten died, combined the two great bands. The Count has no peer, and he will not quit. Still touring America and the world with his band, his music is superlative. Oklahoman Lester Young, playing with Duke Ellington, revolutionized the technique of the alto saxophone. Young Charlie Christian, maker of guitar magic, was moved overnight, by Benny Goodman's scout John Hammond, from an Oklahoma City nightclub to the famed Goodman sextet. With a heritage of black poverty, he died of tuberculosis at age 24.

As fascinating as Oklahoma personalities, the state's place names are equally unique. A town in our panhandle is named Slapout. Guess how it got its name. A crossroads

store there was owned by a man named Johnson. It became commonplace for his pioneer customers, trying to buy some item of merchandise, to be told by Mr. Johnson, "Well, now, I'm just slap out of that." So Johnson's store became known as the slapout store, and the name Slapout stuck to the little town that grew up around the store.

The county seat of Osage County is named Pawhuska, after Osage Chief Pahuchka, whose name meant "white hair." He did not have white hair, but the British soldier he scalped during the Revolutionary War did. The soldier was wearing a white, powdered wig. The Chief's astonishment at how easily this snow white "scalp" came off when he siezed it caused his warrior companions to give him the new name.

Talihina, Choctaw for "iron road," was so named when the Frisco Railroad came through in 1888. Catoosa, northernmost port on the Arkansas River Navigation System, is from the Cherokee Gi-tu-zi, "here live the people of light." Camargo, famed crossing town on the Canadian River, is a Cheyenne word meaning "little dog." Tecumseh, meaning "walks across," is a town name here, as well as the name of the statesman-chief of the Shawnees. Nelagoney, boomtown of the old Osage oilfield, is Osage meaning "good water." Papoose is another boomtown in the same oilfield. You probably know that its translation is "little child" and that it is an Osage word that has come to mean any Indian baby.

The town of Chockie lost half its name. It was originally called ChickieChockie in honor of the two daughters of Captain Charles LeFlore, for whom LeFlore County is named. Captain LeFlore was Choctaw, his wife Chickasaw. They named their first daughter Chickie and their second Chockie. Chickie LeFlore became the wife of Governor Lee Cruce. When she died shortly after the turn of the century Governor Cruce asked that her name be removed from the M. K. & T. depot sign, and the town has since been called Chockie.

Talala is Cherokee word which imitates song of the red bird. Inola means "black fox." Chilocco is from Cherokee "tci-lako," "deer." Ahlosa is "black place." Sasakwa means "goose." Wakita is a Creek expression for "to cry." Wynona is a Sioux word meaning "first born daughter." Tuskahoma is Choctaw for "red warrior." Honobia, pronounced "honubby," means "he went there and killed."

Lake Tenkiller has a common Cherokee name, and there are also Twokillers, Sixkillers, and others, depending on the ancestor's homicidal skill and thirst for blood. Antlers took its name from the Indian custom of hanging a set of antlers on a tree to indicate the presence of a spring nearby. When the railroad came through, a large spring there was so marked. Calumet may make you think of the baking powder, which, like our town, takes its name from the calumet, an Indian peace pipe. And Bowlegs has no reference to anyone's warped anatomy. It is a warping of the name of Captain Billy Bolek, famed Seminole warrior.

The Osage word meaning "we are going home" is "grah-mah." The French mispronounced it "Clarmont," and a prominent Osage chieftan took that name. With a little more distortion, it became Claremore, Will Rogers' home town. Many state names show the French influence. Poteau is French for "post." Vian is from the French "viande" (meat). Early French trappers, working along the Arkansas River, found a salt deposit where they often paused to salt down and preserve their meat. They called the place "Salaison." We call it Sallisaw. So with Spavinaw, which they called "C'pee Vineux" (young growths of trees). The Verdigris River, from "vert gris," (gray green) refers to the color of the boulders along its banks.

The military left its imprint in towns bearing the names of forts once there, and on our creeks and streams. Near every old fort is a Three Mile Creek, a Five Mile Creek, a Six Mile Creek, a convenient way for measuring distance in the days before section line roads or highway markers. There are Oklahoma creeks named Target, Remount, Captain, Quartermaster, Scout, Artillery, and others.

The frontier rancher and cowhand left some names; towns like Mustang, Bray, and Loco, where loco weed, a habit-forming narcotic for horses, once grew thickly along the Chisholm Trail. There are creeks and streams named Cowskin, Trail, Cabin, Dugout, Sourdough, Skeleton, Maverick, Butcher Pen, and Tanyard. Crutcho community is built on land once owned by the Crutch O Ranch, which used a crutch and the letter O as a brand.

The oilrush left names that still bring back the woody, sulphurous smell of crude oil; Barnsdall, Marland, Torpedo, Glenpool, Empire, Oilton. Some names are not what they seem. Kiamichi would seem to be all Indian, but it is a French name for a breed of water bird. Washita, also spelled Ouachita, is not French, but from the Choctaw Owa-chita, an annual tribal "big hunt." Skedee, which sounds like 1920s slang, is named for the "ski-di" (wolf) gens of the Pawnee tribe. And consider the interesting etymology of Skullyville (moneytown). In 1832 the Choctaws were paid their annuities there. The Choctaw word for money is "iskuli." It took some bending to turn iskuli into Skullyville.

Our Spanish heritage shines through at Amorita (little love), Calera (lime kiln), Clarita (little Clara), Eldorado (the golden one), and Orienta, a station on the Kansas City, Mexico and Orient Railroad. Our black heritage includes 28 towns founded by blacks in pioneer Oklahoma; two of them bear the names of black educators, Langston (John M. Langston) and Bookertee (Booker T. Washington).

Soonerland's varied people, living in this varied terrain, take pride in having provided a refuge for Indian people driven from their homelands, for freed-men seeking homes far from Civil War hatreds, for coal mining emigrants (paid $2 a day and always in debt to the company store), for German families in flight from the Kaiser's militarism, for Semitic people who came to forge prosperity out of frugality and hard work. We have had to learn to live and work together.

There are essentially no isolated ethnic groups in Oklahoma except those who, through lack of self-confidence or their own prejudices, choose to isolate themselves. Any racial barriers that exist here are old and infirm. They can be made to crumble before the insistence of those who wish to mingle. We have not achieved a perfect society in which there are no tensions, but we are still trying. Oklahoma's schools were integrated without headline capturing riots. Children of every race attend school together, for still today we are finding room; for homeless Vietnamese, for Asian boat people, for workers from Mexico. Through bilingual education, stressing pride in heritage, we seek to preserve the best of the old cultures and move into the future without losing the birthright of our inheritance from the past.

We have been blessed with mineral wealth and fertile earth. The oil boom days made millionaire philanthropists who not only knew they couldn't take it with them but had no apparent desire to try. Charles Page built Sand Springs Home for widows and orphans in 1907. Tom Gilcrease invested his fortune and his life in the Gilcrease Institute of American History and Art, in Tulsa. This national treasury of art (Remington, Russell, Seltzer, Moran, etc.), pre-history and Indian artifacts from throughout North America and beyond, and documents includes the first letter sent from the New World, dated 1512, written by Christopher Columbus' son Diego. The only known letter written by Hernando De Soto (1535, to Ponce De Leon). The only known certified copy of the Declaration of Independence (sent by Benjamin Franklin to the Minister of Prussia). A certified copy of the Articles of Confederation dated Feb. 14, 1777, and the order that authorized Paul Revere to make his famous "midnight ride."

Frank Phillips established Woolaroc Ranch, Bartlesville, and endowed it with art, a museum, and exotic animals. Activities for young Boy Scouts are generated there. Waite Phillips donated his Philmont Ranch in New Mexico to the Boy Scouts, and his Renaissance mansion, Philbrook, in Tulsa, to the foundation which now oversees its magnificent art collection and educational activities. The Kerr Foundation, the Noble Foundation and others finance agricultural research and development, programs in international understanding, a host of pragmatic and cultural enterprises. The Frank Buttram mansion in Oklahoma City is now the Oklahoma Museum of Art.

Ranchers from 17 states west of the Mississippi River united to build the National Cowboy Hall of Fame and Western Heritage Center at Oklahoma City. Its multimillion dollar collections preserve the American West in paintings, sculptures, dioramas, and annual Western Heritage Awards given in the creative arts.

There are festivals and events to attend, scenic and historic sites to see in every part of Oklahoma. Our multitude of lakes provide for us more shoreline than the Atlantic Coast, and contribute to the system which again makes the Arkansas River navigable. There is no more beautiful river passage anywhere in the world than that between Fort Smith and the Port of Muskogee, especially in autumn or spring. Passage through all locks and dams is free-of-charge.

Oklahoma is a state of busy, hardworking people. It is industrializing, but not pell mell. In areas most attractive to new industry there is often so little unemployment that there is no labor pool from which incoming new industry could draw workers. We who are native here are strongly attached to this land. We are proud of where we've been, enthusiastic about where we're going, and pleased to be located in America's sun belt, which has been targeted by economists as the area of greatest potential in the immediate future development of the nation.

Due to our abundant, year-around sunshine, this is the area where breakthroughs in the production of energy are most likely to come. Pessimists proclaim that solar power, the wind, such sources of energy will never be adequate to replace fossil fuels. Oklahomans have seen so many insoluble problems solved and so many insurmountable barriers surmounted in the growth and development of the oil industry that they have learned how to "hang tough," and are unlikely ever to fully give in to pessimism. Our heritage is religious whatever our race, and we have confidence in our own God-given ingenuity. We believe that the Great Spirit, Dáw-kea, Wa'kon-ta, Dios, however we know Him, will guide our ingenuity to find the way.

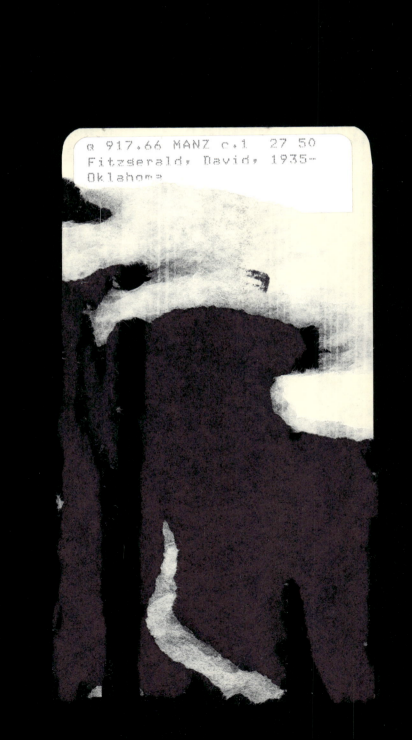